Crafting Your Own Personal Mission Statement

By Amanda Symonds

Contents

What is a personal mission statement and why do you need one?

A personal mission statement is a brief description of what you want to achieve in life. It serves as a guiding principle to help you make decisions that are in line with your goals. When writing a personal mission statement, it is important to consider your values and what you want to achieve. For example, if you value family and community, your mission statement might be to devote your life to serving others. Alternatively, if you value independence and career success, your mission statement might be to become the best at what you do. While a personal mission statement is not set in stone, it can be helpful to have one as it provides a framework for making decisions and setting goals. Ultimately, a personal mission statement is about finding your purpose in life and living in accordance with your values.

What does Steven R Covey say about mission statements?

In his book The 7 Habits of Highly Effective People, Steven R Covey writes that a personal mission statement is "a written expression of your core purpose and guiding principles in life." He goes on to say that a mission statement can help you make decisions that are in line with your goals and values. Ultimately, Covey says that a personal mission statement is about finding your purpose in life and living in accordance with your values.

How to develop your own personal mission statement

A personal mission statement can provide direction and purpose when you feel lost or uncertain. But how do you develop your own mission statement? First, start by thinking about what you want to achieve in life. What are your goals and dreams? What kind of person do you want to be? Once you have a general idea of what you want, start narrowing it down. What are your top priorities? What values do you want to live by? As you hone in on what matters most to you, you'll start to see a theme emerge. That theme is your personal mission statement. It might be something as simple as "To live a life of purpose and joy" or "To be a force for good in the world." Whatever it is, make sure it is something that inspires and motivates you. Once you have developed your mission statement, write it down and refer to it often. Let it guide your decisions and actions, and let it be a source of strength when times are tough. With a clear mission statement, you can achieve anything you set your mind to.

Using ChatGPT to write your personal mission statement

ChatGPT is a powerful AI-based tool that can help to create and enhance your personal mission statement. By asking simple questions, ChatGPT can bring clarity to your life purpose and guide you to make more informed decisions about what actions and goals are most important.

Below are some prompts to get you started using ChatGPT for your mission statement:

1) What is the most important thing in my life?
2) What is the greater good that I want to contribute to?
3) What values do I want to prioritize and embody in my life?
4) What unique skills or passions do I have that could be put towards achieving my mission?
5) How could I bring more creativity, joy and purpose to my mission?

6) What kind of do I want to leave behind

7) What does success mean for me?

8) How can I ensure that my mission is sustainable in the long-term?

9) How can I create a personal action plan based on my mission statement?

10) How will achieving this mission make me feel?

By asking these questions, ChatGPT can help you to craft an inspiring personal mission statement that captures your values, passions and goals. This, in turn, will empower you to live with greater intentionality, purpose and clarity. Through ChatGPT's powerful AI-based platform, you can create a personal mission statement that will enable you to make better decisions, stay focused on your goals and inspire others.

With ChatGPT, crafting a meaningful mission statement is easy and fun.

What should your personal mission statement include?

A personal mission statement is a powerful tool that can help you to focus on what is important in your life. When crafting your mission statement, it is important to consider what you want to achieve and what values are most important to you. Your mission statement should be specific, realistic, and achievable. It should also be something that you are passionate about. In addition, your mission statement should be kept short so that it is easy to remember and recite. By taking the time to create a personal mission statement, you will be better able to focus on your goals and achieve success.

How to stay on track with your personal mission statement

A personal mission statement is a brief summary of your values, goals and aspirations. It is meant to guide your actions and help you make choices that align with your what you want to achieve in life. You can think of your personal mission statement as a road map that will help you stay on track as you work towards your goals.

There are a few things to keep in mind when writing your personal mission statement. First, be sure to articulate your values clearly. What is important to you? What do you stand for? Once you have articulated your values, you can start setting goals that align with them. Be specific about what you want to achieve and set a timeline for yourself. Finally, don't be afraid to revise your mission statement as your values and goals change over time. What matters today may not matter as much tomorrow, and that's okay. Your personal mission statement should be a living document that evolves as you do.

Examples of personal mission statements

"To laugh often and much; to win the respect of intelligent people and the affection of children; to earn the appreciation of honest critics and endure the betrayal of false friends; to appreciate beauty, to find the best in others; to leave the world a bit better, whether by a healthy child, a garden patch or a redeemed social condition; to know even one life has breathed easier because you have lived. This is to have succeeded." - Ralph Waldo Emerson

"My mission in life is not merely to survive, but to thrive; and to do so with some passion, some compassion, some humor, and some style." - Maya Angelou

"To live each day as if it were my last, to love deeply and passionately, to dance like nobody's watching, to sing like nobody's listening, and to always keep the faith." - Maya Angelou

"I want to live my life in such a way that when I get out of bed in the morning, the devil says, 'aw shit, he's up.'" - Steve Maraboli, Life, the Truth, and Being Free

"Be the change you want to see in the world." - Mahatma Gandhi

"My mission is to help people be their best and live their lives to the fullest." - Tony Robbins

"To live a life of purpose and meaning, to be a force for good in the world, and to make a positive difference in the lives of others." - Oprah Winfrey

"To build a better world through my work, to contribute to making it a place where everyone can live with dignity, freedom, democracy, justice, and peace." - Kofi Annan

"My mission is not to be perfect but to be whole, to accept myself for who I am and not to judge myself for the things I am not." - Marianne Williamson

"To make a difference in the lives of others by using my talents and resources to help them reach their potential." - Bill Gates

"To bring hope to the suffering, joy to the sorrowful , and love to the brokenhearted." - Mother Teresa

"To be a force for good in the world, to help others, and to make a difference." - Barack Obama

"To use my talents and resources to make a positive difference in the lives of others." - Warren Buffett

"I want to make a difference. I want to help make the world a better place." - Mark Zuckerberg

"My mission is to inspire others to live their dreams and be the best they can be." - Les Brown

"To make a difference in the lives of those around me and to create a legacy that lasts long after I'm gone." - Kobe Bryant

"I want to inspire people. I want to show them that anything's possible if they just try." - Michael Jordan

"To use my talents and resources to make a positive difference in the lives of others." - Tiger Woods

"To be a role model and an inspiration to others, especially young people." - Serena Williams

Is there a formula?

As you can see, all successful mission statements share some common elements. They are specific, realistic, achievable, and inspiring. They also reflect the values and goals of the person who created them. Keep these things in mind as you develop your own personal mission statement.

Your personal mission statement is a powerful tool that can help you to focus on what is important in your life. When crafting your mission statement, it is important to consider what you want to achieve and what values are most important to you. Your mission statement should be specific, realistic, and achievable. It should also be something that you are passionate about.

In addition, your mission statement should be kept short so that it is easy to remember and recite. By taking the time to create a personal mission statement, you will be better able to focus on your goals.

A personal mission statement is a short, powerful declaration of your core values and interests. By articulating your intentions, a personal mission statement can help you maintain focus and stay on track, both professionally and personally. While there is no one-size-fits-all formula for writing a personal mission statement, there are a few elements that are essential:

First, your mission statement should be clear and concise.

Second, it should be specific to you and reflect your unique talents and goals.

Third, it should inspire you to take action and provide guidance when you face difficult choices.

That's right, it should help you say NO to things that don't align with your values and goals.

Fourth, it should be flexible enough to change as you grow and evolve.

Your personal mission statement is not meant to be set in stone, but rather should be revised as your needs and interests change over time.

Finally, a personal mission statement should be something you read and regularly recite, in order to keep it top of mind.

By reading and repeating your mission statement often, you will be better able to make choices that align with your goals, both in your professional and personal life.

Now it's your turn! Write your own personal mission statement using the tips above. Remember, there is no one right way to do this. The most important thing is that your statement reflects your unique goals, values, and talents.

By taking the time to develop a personal mission statement, you can live a life that is in alignment with your values and goals.

"Your personal mission statement is like a road map for your life. It sets out where you want to go and how you're going to get there." -Tony Robbins

"The best way to find out what we truly need in life is to examine what we truly want." - Richard Bach, author of Jonathan Livingston Seagull

"The only way to do great work is to love what you do." - Steve Jobs

"Your time is limited, don't waste it living someone else's life." - Steve Jobs

"If you don't design your own life plan, chances are you'll fall into someone else's plan. And guess what they have planned for you? Not much!" - Jim Rohn

Using your personal mission statement to choose your career

Now that you know how to write a personal mission statement, it's time to put it into action. Your personal mission statement can be a powerful tool to help you make difficult choices, both in your professional and personal life.

When it comes to your career, your personal mission statement can help you to identify your long-term goals and make choices that will help you to achieve them.

For example, if your goal is to become a successful writer, your personal mission statement might look something like this:

"I am a writer who uses my words to inspire and empower others. I write to make a difference in the world, and I only work on projects that I am passionate about."

By articulating your goals and values, you can make sure that your career choices are in line with what you want to achieve. As an author, I have decided only to work on projects that I am passionate about because that is what will make a difference in the world to me.

For example, if you're a writer who is looking for a way to make a difference in the world, you might want to consider working on a project that focuses on social justice or environmentalism.

By keeping your goals and values top of mind, you can make sure that you're always moving in the right direction.

Feeling stuck and need career advice?

Your personal mission statement can also help you when you're feeling stuck or uncertain about your next career move. If you're not sure whether to take a new job or pursue a different opportunity, ask yourself how the decision will impact your long-term goals.

For example, if you're considering taking a job that pays well but isn't in line with your values, you might want to ask yourself whether the job is worth sacrificing your happiness and fulfilment.

"Remember, you have been criticizing yourself for years and it hasn't worked. Try approving of yourself and see what happens." - Louise Hay

"The only person who is responsible for the quality of your life is you." - Randy Pausch, author of The Last Lecture

"You are never too old to set new goals or to dream a new dream." - C.S. Lewis

If you read your personal mission statement and think about how it applies in several job fields, it will open you up to considering many more job options. This is particularly important if you are early in your career. You want to keep your options open until you find the right fit.

Considering what subjects you excel in at school is half of the job search. The other half is figuring out what you like to do. If you are not 100% set on a career, your personal mission statement can help you to identify your passions and figure out which job will be the best fit for you.

For example, if you're passionate about writing and helping others, a career in copywriting, marketing, or even teaching might be a good fit for you. You may find that you move around in your career a bit before you find the right niche, and that's OK! As long as you're moving in the right direction, you're on the right track.

"Your work is going to fill a large part of your life, and the only way to be truly satisfied is to do what you believe is great work. And the only way to do great work is to love what you do. If you haven't found it yet, keep looking. Don't settle. As with all matters of the heart, you'll know when you find it." - Steve Jobs

"Find something you're passionate about and stay tremendously interested in it." - Julia Child

"The most important thing is to enjoy your life - to be happy - it's all that matters." - Dalai Lama

"Do what you love, and the money will follow." - Marsha Sinetar

"The best way to find out what you want to do with your life is by exploring the world and doing new things." - Richard Branson

"Your career will never wake up one day and tell you that it doesn't love you anymore." - Harvey Mackay

"Do what you feel in your heart to be right – for you'll be criticized anyway. You'll be damned if you do, and damned if you don't." - Eleanor Roosevelt

What is your personal branding statement?

Your personal mission statement can also be used as your personal branding statement. A personal branding statement is a short, clear sentence that describes who you are as a professional. It should highlight your strengths and accomplishments, and it should be memorable.

Your personal branding statement might be something like, "I am an experienced copywriter who helps businesses to connect with their customers through compelling storytelling."

Think about how you want to be perceived by others, and use your personal mission statement to craft a personal branding statement that will help you to achieve your goals.

"Your personal brand is the single most important investment you can make in your career." - Forbes

"A strong personal brand will make you more visible, better qualified, and more likely to get the job or promotion you want." - Entrepreneur

"Your personal brand is what people say about you when you're not in the room." - Jeff Bezos

"People are attracted to authenticity, not perfection." - Brené Brown

"Be yourself; everyone else is already taken." - Oscar Wilde

"To thine own self be true." - Shakespeare

Where do I use my personal mission statement?

Now that you have your personal mission statement, it's time to put it to work! Here are some ways to do that:

1. Use it as a filter when considering job opportunities.

2. Incorporate it into your LinkedIn profile, resume and cover letter.

3. Share it with your friends, family, and mentors to get their input and feedback.

4. Use it as a guide when making decisions about your career.

5. Revisit it periodically to make sure it still reflects your goals and values.

Writing a personal mission statement is an important exercise to help you figure out what you want to do with your life. But it's only the first step. Once you have your statement, put it to work and use it as a guide to help you make decisions about your career. With a clear personal mission, you can achieve great things!

Now that you have your personal mission statement, it's time to put it into action!

Setting goals

The first step is to set goals that align with your mission statement. Once you have a clear idea of what you want to achieve, you can start working towards it. Some things to keep in mind when setting goals:

 1. Make sure your goals are specific, measurable, achievable, relevant and time-bound. This will help you to stay on track and make progress towards your goals.

2. Write down your goals and refer to them often. This will help to keep you accountable and motivated.

3. Share your goals with others who can support you on your journey.

4. Be flexible and willing to adjust your goals as you learn more about what you want and what's possible.

5. Celebrate your progress along the way!

"A goal without a plan is just a wish." - Antoine de Saint-Exupéry

"The trouble with not having a goal is that you can spend your life running up and down the field and never score." - Bill Copeland

"The best way to make your dreams come true is to wake up." - J.M. Power

"If you want to live a happy life, tie it to a goal, not to people or things." - Albert Einstein

"People with goals succeed because they know where they're going." - Earl Nightingale

"The only way to do great work is to love what you do." - Steve Jobs

"If you can dream it, you can do it." - Walt Disney

Examples of personal mission statements for accountants

"I am dedicated to providing accurate and reliable financial information that helps my clients make informed decisions. I am committed to maintaining the highest standards of integrity and professionalism in my work."

"I am a passionate about helping businesses grow and succeed. I use my skills and knowledge to provide insightful advice and guidance that helps my clients make sound financial decisions."

"I am is committed to providing excellent service to my clients. I strive to exceed their expectations by providing quality work and timely results."

Examples of personal mission statements for actors

"I am an actor who uses my talents to entertain and inspire others. I strive to create work that is meaningful and impactful, and I always aim to leave my audience feeling enriched."

"I am a dedicated artist who is constantly seeking new challenges. I thrive on taking risks and pushing myself outside of my comfort zone, and I am always looking for ways to grow and evolve as an actor."

"I am an actor who is committed to telling stories that resonate with audiences. I choose projects that inspire me, and I strive to create characters that people can relate to and connect with."

Examples of personal mission statements for artists

"I am an artist who is passionate about using my work to express myself and connect with others. I strive to create pieces that are beautiful and thought-provoking, and I hope to inspire others to see the world in new and exciting ways."

"I am an artist who is dedicated to creating meaningful and impactful work. I choose projects that are important to me, and I strive to use my art to make a difference in the world."

"I am an artist who is committed to excellence in everything I do. I strive for perfection in my work, and I always aim to produce the best possible results."

Examples of personal mission statements for authors

"I am an author who writes to entertain, inform, and inspire others. I strive to create work that is entertaining and enjoyable to read, while also providing valuable information and insights."

"I am an author who is dedicated to creating quality content that educates and informs my readers. I only write about topics that I am passionate about, and I always aim to provide accurate and reliable information."

"I am an author who writes to make a difference in the world. I choose projects that are important to me, and I use my words to raise awareness and promote positive change."

Examples of personal mission statements for builders

"I am a builder who is committed to creating quality homes that families can enjoy for years to come. I use my skills and knowledge to construct homes that are both beautiful and functional, and I take pride in my workmanship."

"I am a builder who is passionate about creating homes that are energy efficient and sustainable. I use the latest technologies and materials to construct homes that are built to last, and I always aim to exceed my clients' expectations."

"I am a builder who is dedicated to providing my clients with the best possible service. I strive to create a hassle-free experience for my clients, from start to finish, and I always put their needs first."

Examples of personal mission statements for business owners

"I am a business owner who is passionate about helping other businesses succeed. I use my skills and knowledge to provide insights and guidance that helps my clients reach their goals."

"I am a business owner who is committed to providing quality products and services that meet the needs of my customers. I strive to exceed their expectations with every interaction, and I always aim to deliver the best possible experience."

"I am a business owner who is dedicated to building long-term relationships with my clients. I work hard to provide them with the best possible service, and I always aim to be a trusted partner that they can rely on."

Examples of personal mission statements for business leaders

"I am a business leader who is committed to building a successful and sustainable company. I use my skills and knowledge to make strategic decisions that help my business grow and thrive."

"I am a business leader who is passionate about creating an organization that is built on integrity and fairness. I strive to create a workplace where everyone can thrive, and I always aim to treat my employees with respect."

"I am a business leader who is dedicated to making a positive impact in the world. I choose projects that are important to me, and I use my platform to raise awareness and promote positive change."

Examples of personal mission statements for chefs

"I am a chef who is passionate about creating delicious and healthy food. I use the freshest ingredients and cook with care to create meals that are nourishing and satisfying."

"I am a chef who is committed to providing my guests with an amazing dining experience. I create unique and flavorful dishes, and I always aim to leave my guests wanting more."

"I am a chef who is dedicated to providing healthy and nutritious food to my community. I cook with local ingredients and seasonal produce to create dishes that are both delicious and healthy."

"I am a chef who is passionate about using my culinary skills to make a difference in the world. "To use my knowledge and skills to benefit my diners and help them enjoy their meal."

Examples of personal mission statements for cleaners

"I am a cleaner who is committed to providing a clean and safe environment for everyone. I use the latest cleaning technologies and products to ensure that all areas are clean and free of contaminants."

"I am a cleaner who is passionate about making a difference in the world. I choose to use products that are environmentally friendly and organize when I clean to promote positive work environments."

"I am a cleaner who is dedicated to providing quality cleaning and organizational services that meet the needs of my clients. I strive to exceed their expectations with every interaction, and I always aim to deliver the best possible experience."

"I am a cleaner who is committed to providing clean and safe environments for all. I use my knowledge and skills to benefit my community, and I always aim to make a positive impact."

Examples of personal mission statements for consultants

"I am a consultant who is passionate about helping my clients reach their goals. I use my skills and knowledge to provide insights and guidance that helps them succeed."

"I am a consultant who is committed to providing quality services that meet the needs of my clients. I strive to exceed their expectations with every interaction, and I always aim to deliver the best possible experience."

"I am a consultant who is dedicated to helping my clients achieve their objectives. I work hard to provide them with the best possible service, and I always aim to be a trusted partner that they can rely on."

"I am a consultant who is committed to making a positive impact in the world. I choose projects that are important to me, and I use my platform to raise awareness and promote positive change."

"To help clients reach their goals by providing quality insights and guidance."

Examples of personal mission statements for counsellors

"I am a counsellor who is dedicated to helping my clients work through their challenges and achieve their goals. I provide a safe and supportive environment where they can explore their feelings and experiences."

"To provide a safe, non-judgmental space for clients to explore their thoughts and feelings."

"To help clients find clarity and direction in their lives."

"To empower clients to make positive changes in their lives."

"To support clients as they navigate through difficult life transitions."

"To help clients heal from past traumas and learn to live more fully in the present."

"To provide clients with tools and resources to manage anxiety, stress, and other mental health challenges."

"To assist clients in exploring their values and how they can align their lives with those values."

"To help clients create more fulfilling and meaningful lives."

"To support clients as they strive to reach their personal and professional goals."

"To help clients overcome obstacles and achieve their desired outcomes."

"To provide clients with the tools and resources they need to make positive changes in their lives."

Examples of personal mission statements for coaches

"I am a coach who is passionate about helping my clients reach their potential. I use my knowledge and experience to guide them through their journey and help them achieve their goals."

"I am a coach who is dedicated to helping my clients grow and develop. I work with them to identify their strengths and weaknesses, and I help them create a plan to improve their skills and abilities."

"I am a coach who is committed to helping my clients reach their goals. I work with them to create a plan of action and provide support and guidance as they work towards their goals."

"I am a coach who is dedicated to helping my clients reach their potential. I work with them to identify their goals and create a plan to help them achieve success. I also provide support and resources to help them along the way."

"To help my clients reach their goals by providing quality coaching services."

"To use my knowledge and skills to benefit my clients and help them achieve success."

"To be a trusted resource for my clients and help them navigate the coaching process."

"To always provide quality service and care to my clients".

Examples of personal mission statements for doctors

"I am a doctor who is committed to providing quality care for my patients. I strive to exceed their expectations and provide them with the best possible experience."

"I am a doctor who is dedicated to helping my patients achieve their health goals. I work hard to provide them with the best possible care, and I always aim to be a trusted partner that they can rely on."

"I am a doctor who is passionate about helping my patients lead healthy and fulfilling lives and adapt to aging. I work with them to identify their health goals and create a plan to help them achieve success in weight loss or fitness.

"To save lives and help others by providing quality medical care."

"To use my knowledge and skills to benefit my patients and help them achieve good health."

"To be a trusted resource for my patients and help them navigate the healthcare system."

"To always provide quality care and compassion to my patients".

Examples of personal mission statements for engineers

"I am an engineer who is committed to using my skills to benefit society. I work hard to develop innovative solutions that make a positive impact on the world."

"I am an engineer who is dedicated to developing sustainable and environmentally friendly solutions. I work hard to create buildings/structures that are safe for people, energy efficient and not wasting resources from the planet."

"I am an engineer who is passionate about using my skills to improve the world. I work with communities to identify their needs and develop solutions that make a positive impact."

"To use my engineering skills to benefit society and make a positive impact on the world."

"To develop innovative, sustainable and environmentally friendly solutions."

"To be a trusted resource for communities and help them navigate the development process."

"To use my knowledge and skills to improve the world we live in."

"To help others by using my talents to make a difference in their lives."

"To make a positive impact on the world through my work."

"To inspire others to never give up on their dreams and pursue their passions."

"To use my knowledge and skills to make a difference in the world."

"To be a force for good and bring about positive change."

"My mission is to use my knowledge and skills to improve the world we live in."

Examples of personal mission statements for entrepreneurs

"I am an entrepreneur who is committed to making a difference. I work hard to create innovative products and services that improve people's lives."

"I am an entrepreneur who is dedicated to helping others achieve their dreams. I work with them to identify their goals and create a plan to help them achieve success. I also provide support and resources to help them along the way."

"I am an entrepreneur who is passionate about making a difference in the world. I work hard to create products and services that improve people's lives and make a positive impact on society."

"To use my entrepreneurial skills to benefit society and make a positive impact on the world."

"To create innovative products and services that improve people's lives."

"To be a trusted resource for entrepreneurs and help them navigate the business world."

"To use my knowledge and skills to improve the world we live in."

"To create something that lasts and makes a positive impact on the world."

"To inspire others to pursue their passions and never give up on their dreams."

"To build a company that is not just about making money, but about making a difference."

"To change the world for the better through my business."

"To use my talents and abilities to help others achieve their goals."

"To create something that makes people's lives better and brings them joy."

Examples of personal mission statements for farmers

"I am a farmer who is committed to producing quality food. I work hard to provide healthy and nutritious food for my community."

"I am a farmer who is dedicated to sustainable agriculture. I work hard to protect the environment and preserve our natural resources."

To use my skills as a farmer to benefit my community and make a positive impact on the world.

To produce quality food that is healthy and nutritious.

To practice sustainable agriculture and protect our natural resources.

"To help others by providing quality food and products."

"To use my knowledge and skills to benefit my community and help them maintain a healthy lifestyle."

"To be a trusted resource for my community and help them have access to fresh food."

Examples of personal mission statements for financial planners

"I am a financial planner who is committed to helping people achieve their financial goals. I work hard to provide advice and resources that help them make sound financial decisions."

"I am a financial planner who is dedicated to helping people secure their financial future. I work hard with them to develop a plan that meets their individual needs and goals."

"I am a financial planner who is passionate about helping people improve their financial situation. I work hard to provide advice and resources that can help them make better financial choices."

To use my knowledge and skills as a financial planner to benefit my clients and help them achieve their goals.

To provide advice and resources that help people make sound financial decisions.

To be a trusted resource for my clients and help them navigate their financial future.

"To help my clients reach their financial goals by providing quality planning and advice."

"To use my knowledge and skills to benefit my clients and help them achieve success."

"To be a trusted resource for my clients and help them navigate the financial planning process."

Examples of personal mission statements for funeral directors

"I am a funeral director who is committed to providing quality services. I work hard to provide compassionate and professional care to families during their time of need."

"I am a funeral director who is dedicated to helping families through the grieving process. I work hard to provide guidance and support during this difficult time."

"I am a funeral director who is passionate about helping families honor their loved ones. I work hard to provide quality services that reflect the unique needs and desires of each family."

To use my knowledge and skills as a funeral director to benefit the families I serve.

To provide quality services that reflect the unique needs, religious beliefs and desires of each family.

To be a trusted resource for families during the grieving process.

"To help families through the grieving process by providing quality services."

"To use my knowledge and skills to benefit the families I serve."

"To help families through one of the most difficult times in their lives."

"To provide support and guidance to families during the grieving process."

"To create a meaningful and personalized funeral service that celebrates the life of the deceased."

"To help families through the funeral planning process with compassion and care."

"To provide a shoulder to lean on during one of the most difficult times in a person's life."

"To be a source of support and comfort for grieving families."

Examples of personal mission statements for gardeners

"I am a gardener who is committed to helping people create beautiful outdoor spaces. I work hard to provide quality plants and products that help them achieve their vision."

"I am a gardener who is dedicated to helping people connect with nature. I work hard to provide plants and products that help them create a space that is both beautiful and inviting."

"I am a gardener who is passionate about helping people create healthy outdoor spaces. I work hard to provide quality plants and products that help them achieve their goals."

To use my knowledge and skills as a gardener to benefit the people I serve.

To provide quality plants and products that help people create beautiful, healthy outdoor spaces.

To be a trusted resource for people who want to connect with nature.

"To help people create beautiful outdoor spaces by providing quality plants and products."

"To use my knowledge and skills as a gardener to benefit the people I serve."

"To help others by providing quality gardening services."

"To use my knowledge and skills to benefit my clients and help them maintain their homes."

"To be a trusted resource for my clients and help them keep their gardens beautiful."

"To always provide quality service and care to my clients."

Examples of personal mission statements for hairdressers

"I am a hairdresser who is committed to helping my clients look and feel their best. I work hard to provide quality services that reflect their individual style."

"I am a hairdresser who is dedicated to providing my clients with the best possible experience. I work hard to provide quality services that are both professional and personal."

"I am a hairdresser who is passionate about helping my clients feel beautiful. I work hard to provide quality services that reflect their individual style and personality."

To use my knowledge and skills as a hairdresser to benefit the people I serve.

"To help others feel good about themselves by providing quality hair care services."

"To use my knowledge and skills to benefit my clients and help them look and feel their best."

"To be a trusted resource for my clients and help them maintain their appearance."

"To always provide quality service and care to my clients."

Examples of personal mission statements for hospital staff

"I am a hospital staff member who is committed to providing quality care for my patients. I work hard to ensure that they receive the best possible treatment."

"I am a hospital staff member who is dedicated to providing compassionate care for my patients. I work hard to ensure that they receive the best possible treatment."

"To provide quality care and service to our patients and their families."

"To use our knowledge and skills to benefit our patients and help them recover."

"To be a trusted resource for our patients and their families and help them navigate the healthcare system."

"To always provide quality care and compassion to our patients."

Examples of personal mission statements for IT technicians

"I am an IT technician who is committed to providing quality service for my clients. I work hard to ensure that they receive the best possible support."

"To help businesses by providing quality IT services."

"To use my knowledge and skills to benefit my clients and help them achieve their goals."

"To be a trusted resource for my clients and help them maintain their systems."

"To always provide quality service and care to my clients."

"My mission is to help businesses by providing information and updates to clients to keep their data safe and secure".

Examples of personal mission statements for lawyers

"I am a lawyer who is committed to justice for my clients. I work hard to ensure that they receive the best possible outcome."

"To provide quality legal services to my clients."

"To use my knowledge and skills to benefit my clients and help them receive the best possible outcome."

"To be a trusted resource for my clients and help them navigate the legal system."

"To always provide quality service and care to my clients."

"To help others by using my knowledge and skills to make a difference in their lives."

"To fight for justice and equality for all."

"To stand up for the rights of others and ensure that everyone is treated fairly."

"To use my talents and abilities to help those who need it most."

"To make a difference in the world by using my knowledge and skills to help others."

Examples of personal mission statements for librarians

"I am a librarian who is committed to providing access to information for all. I work hard to ensure that everyone has the opportunity to learn and grow."

"To provide quality library services to my community."

"To use my knowledge and skills to benefit my community and help them access the information they need."

"To help others find the information they need and improve their lives."

"To promote literacy and a love of learning."

"To be a trusted resource for my community and help them grow and thrive."

Examples of personal mission statements for marriage celebrants

"I am a marriage celebrant who is committed to helping couples celebrate their love for each other. I work hard to ensure that their special day is perfect."

"To help couples celebrate their love for each other and create lasting memories."

"To use my knowledge and skills to benefit my clients and help them create the perfect wedding day."

"To be a trusted resource for my clients and help them plan their dream wedding."

"To always provide quality service and care to my clients."

"To help couples celebrate their love for each other and create lasting memories."

"To help couples create lasting memories of their special day."

"To officiate ceremonies that are personal, unique, and reflect the couple's values and love for each other."

"To be a calm and supportive presence on one of the most important days of a couple's life."

"To create a ceremony that is a beautiful and joyous reflection of the couple's love for each other."

"To help couples start their married life together on a strong foundation."

Examples of personal mission statements for musicians

"To make beautiful music that touches the hearts of all who hear it."

"To share my gift of music with the world and bring joy to others."

"To use my talents to lift up others and create positive change in the world."

"To inspire others with my music and help them find their own voices."

"To create music that is a force for good in the world."

Examples of personal mission statements for midwives

"I am a midwife who is committed to providing quality care for mothers and babies. I work hard to ensure that they receive the best possible care."

"To provide quality care for mothers and babies and help them thrive."

"To use my knowledge and skills to benefit mothers and babies and help them receive the best possible care."

"To be a trusted resource for mothers and babies and help them navigate the healthcare system."

"To make a difference in the lives of others by providing quality care and compassion to mothers and babies."

"To help others by providing quality midwifery care and services."

"To use my knowledge and skills to benefit my clients and help them during one of the most important times in their lives."

"To be a trusted resource for my clients and help them navigate the birthing process."

"To always provide quality service and care to my clients."

Examples of personal mission statements for models

"To inspire others through my modeling."

"To use my talents to benefit the fashion industry and help it progress."

"To be a trusted resource for the fashion industry and help it connect with the public."

"To always provide quality entertainment and care to those who follow my modeling career."

Examples of personal mission statements for nurses

"I am a nurse who is committed to providing quality care for my patients. I work hard to ensure that they receive the best possible treatment."

"To provide quality care for my patients and help them recover and heal."

"To use my knowledge and skills to benefit my patients and help them receive the best possible care."

"To be a trusted resource for my patients and help them navigate the healthcare system."

"To always provide quality care and compassion to my patients."

"To make a difference in the lives of others by providing quality care and compassion."

"To provide care and support to those in need and be a source of strength for them."

"To always try to see the best in people and help them through their challenges."

"To use my knowledge and skills to improve the health and well-being of others."

"To make a difference in the world by helping others in whatever way I can."

"To be a force for good and bring healing and hope to those I encounter."

Examples of personal mission statements for pathologists

"To be a trusted resource for my patients and help them navigate the healthcare system."

"To use my knowledge and skills to benefit my clients and help them understand their health."

"To be a trusted resource for my clients and help them navigate the healthcare system."

"To always provide quality service and care to my clients."

Examples of personal mission statements for police officer

"To keep the peace and protect the public."

"To serve and protect my community."

"To uphold the law and maintain order."

"To always put the safety of others first."

"To serve and protect my community."

"To ensure that everyone in my community feels safe and secure."

"To use my knowledge and skills to benefit my community and help keep it a great place to live."

Examples of personal mission statements for politicians

"To make a difference in the world by working to improve the lives of others."

"To use my knowledge and skills to benefit my community and help make it a better place to live."

"To work tirelessly to make the world a better place for future generations."

"To be a voice for the voiceless and fight for those who cannot fight for themselves."

"To stand up for what is right, even when it is not popular."

"To always be honest and transparent in my work."

"To help my constituents by providing quality representation."

"To use my knowledge and skills to benefit my community and help them navigate the political system."

"To be a trusted resource for my community and help them achieve their goals."

"To always provide quality service and care to my community."

Examples of personal mission statements for plumbers

"To help others by providing quality plumbing services and solutions."

"To be a trusted resource for my clients and help them maintain their homes."

"To use my knowledge and skills to benefit my clients and help them achieve their goals."

"To always provide quality service and care to my clients."

Examples of personal mission statements for realtors

"To help my clients navigate the real estate market and find their perfect home."

"To use my knowledge and skills to benefit my clients and help them achieve their real estate goals."

"To help people find their perfect home and make their dreams come true."

"To provide quality service and care to my clients throughout their real estate journey."

"To be a trusted resource for my clients and help them navigate the real estate process."

"To use my knowledge and skills to benefit my clients and help them achieve their goals."

Examples of personal mission statements for scientists

"To use my knowledge and skills to benefit society and make the world a better place."

"To make a difference in the world by helping others in whatever way I can."

"To help others by providing quality scientific research."

"To use my knowledge and skills to benefit society and help it progress."

"To be a trusted resource for society and help it understand the scientific process."

"To always provide quality research and care to those who follow my scientific career."

Examples of personal mission statements for soldiers

"To defend my country and its people."

"To serve and protect my community."

"To use my knowledge and skills to benefit my country and its people."

"To help protect others by serving my country."

"To use my skills and training to benefit my unit and help it succeed."

"To be a trusted resource for my unit and help them complete their mission."

Examples of personal mission statements for taxi drivers

"To help people get where they need to go."

"To provide quality service and care to my passengers."

"To be a trusted resource for my passengers and help them navigate the city."

"To use my knowledge and skills to benefit my passengers and help them get to appointments on time."

"To help others by providing quality transportation services."

"To use my knowledge and skills to benefit my clients and help them get where they need to go."

"To be a trusted resource for my clients and help them navigate the city."

"To always provide quality service and care to my clients."

Examples of personal mission statements for teachers

"To help my students reach their potential and succeed in life."

"To make a difference in the lives of my students by providing them with the knowledge and skills they need to succeed."

"To inspire my students to pursue their dreams and never give up."

"To instil a love of learning in my students and help them reach their full potential."

"To be a positive influence in my students' lives and help them become the best people they can be."

"To prepare my students for the future and help them achieve their goals."

"To use my knowledge and skills to make a positive impact on my students' lives."

"To create a safe and supportive learning environment for all students."

"To help students discover their talents and passions."

"To teach students to think critically and problem-solve."

"To prepare students for success in the real world."

Examples of personal mission statements for tradespeople

"To help others by providing quality services and solutions."

"To use my knowledge and skills to benefit my clients and help them achieve their goals."

"To be a trusted resource for my clients and help them maintain their homes."

"To always provide quality service and care to my clients."

Examples of personal mission statements for valets

"To help others by providing quality parking services."

"To use my knowledge and skills to benefit my clients and help them park their cars."

"To be a trusted resource for my clients and help them navigate the parking lot."

"To always provide quality service and care to my clients."

Examples of personal mission statements for veterinarians

"To be a trusted resource for pet owners and help them care for their animals."

"To always provide quality medical care and service to our furry patients."

"To help animals by providing quality medical care."

"To use my knowledge and skills to benefit society and help protect animal welfare."

"To be a trusted resource for society and help it understand the importance of animal health."

"To inspire others to pursue their dreams of becoming a veterinarian."

Examples of personal mission statements for waiters / waitresses

"To provide quality service and care to my guests, particularly those with dietary needs."

"To be a trusted resource for my guests and help them select from the menu."

"To always provide quality service and care to my guests."

"To use my culinary knowledge and wine selection skills to benefit my guests and help them enjoy their meal."

"To help families celebrate special occasions by creating a memorable dining experience."

"To be the best server that I can be and to provide quality service with a smile."

"To always go above and beyond for my guests."

"To provide top-notch service that exceeds expectations."

"To make every guest feel like they are my only guest."

"To provide an exceptional dining experience for every guest, every time."

"To be a team player and contribute to a positive work environment."

"To build relationships with guests and create regulars."

"To make a difference in the lives of my guests by providing them with quality service and care."

"To be a positive influence in the lives of my co-workers and help them reach their potential."

Examples of personal mission statements for yoga teachers

"To help people connect with their bodies and minds to achieve greater peace and balance in their lives."

"To inspire others to live a healthier lifestyle ."

"To help people discover their own strength, flexibility, and power."

"To provide a space for people to relax, de-stress, and connect with their breath."

"To create a community of supportive and like-minded individuals."

"To be a positive influence in the lives of my students and help them reach their potential."

"To empower others to lead healthier and more balanced lives."

"To help people find inner peace and contentment."

"To provide a space for people of all levels to come and practice yoga."

"To help people feel better in their bodies and minds."

"To offer a sanctuary for people to discover their own personal strength and power."

"To encourage people to lead healthier and more balanced lives."

"To help others find peace, balance, and joy in their lives through yoga."

"To share the gift of yoga with as many people as possible and help them improve their lives."

"To use my knowledge and skills to help others achieve their goals."

"To be a force for good and inspire others to do the same."

"To always try to see the best in people and be kind, compassionate, and understanding."

"I am grateful for all that I have been given in life and will strive to do everything I can to make the world a better place."

"My mission is to help others find peace, balance, and joy in their lives through yoga."

Creating a visual personal mission statement

You can also create a visual personal mission statement to help you remember and live by your goals. This could be a collage, vision board, or even just a list of words or phrases that inspire you. You can hang your visual personal mission statement where you will see it every day to remind you of what you are working towards.

Some ideas for creating a visual personal mission statement include:

-Using inspiring words or quotes

-Including images that represent your goals and dreams

-Making a collage of pictures that make you happy or inspire you

-Creating a vision board with images and words that represent your ideal life

-Drawing or painting a picture that represents your personal mission statement

-Writing your personal mission statement in calligraphy or another visually appealing way

-Decorating a box or jar with your visual personal mission statement and filling it with things that inspire you (like quotes, tickets to your favorite place, or pictures of loved ones)

No matter what form your visual personal mission statement takes, make sure it is something that you will enjoy looking at and that will remind you of your goals.

Summary

Remember, there is no one right way to write a personal mission statement. The most important thing is that it reflects your unique talents, goals, and values. With that in mind, here are a few tips to get you started:

1. Keep it short and sweet. A personal mission statement should be concise and easy to remember.

2. Be specific. Reflect on what you want to achieve and what values are most important to you.

3. Make it realistic. While your mission statement should be aspirational, it should also be achievable.

4. Keep it flexible. Allow your mission statement to change as you grow and evolve.

5. Recite it often. In order to keep your mission statement top of mind, read it aloud regularly.

Conclusion

Your personal mission statement is a reflection of your values, career goals and aspirations. It acts as a compass to help you stay on track when life gets overwhelming and you feel like you're losing sight of what's important. If you don't have a personal mission statement yet, follow the steps outlined in this guide to develop one that works for you. And if you need some inspiration, read through some examples of powerful personal mission statements from successful people across various industries. Remember, your personal mission statement should evolve as you do, so revisit it often and make adjustments as needed.

Other books by Amanda Symonds

Power Phrases for Performance Reviews

End Writer's Block

Secret AI Ghostwriter

300 Online Dating Profile Phrases

Create Your Own Escape Room

www.ingramcontent.com/pod-product-compliance
Lightning Source LLC
Chambersburg PA
CBHW071715210326

41597CB00017B/2494